Hawaii FAVORITES

To access audio visit:
www.halleonard.com/mylibrary
Enter Code
2475-4128-5418-8663

Ukulele performed by Curt Mychael

Tracking, mixing, and mastering by Jake Johnson and Chris Kringel

ISBN 978-1-4234-9071-5

Aloha Oe

Words and Music by Queen Liliuokalani

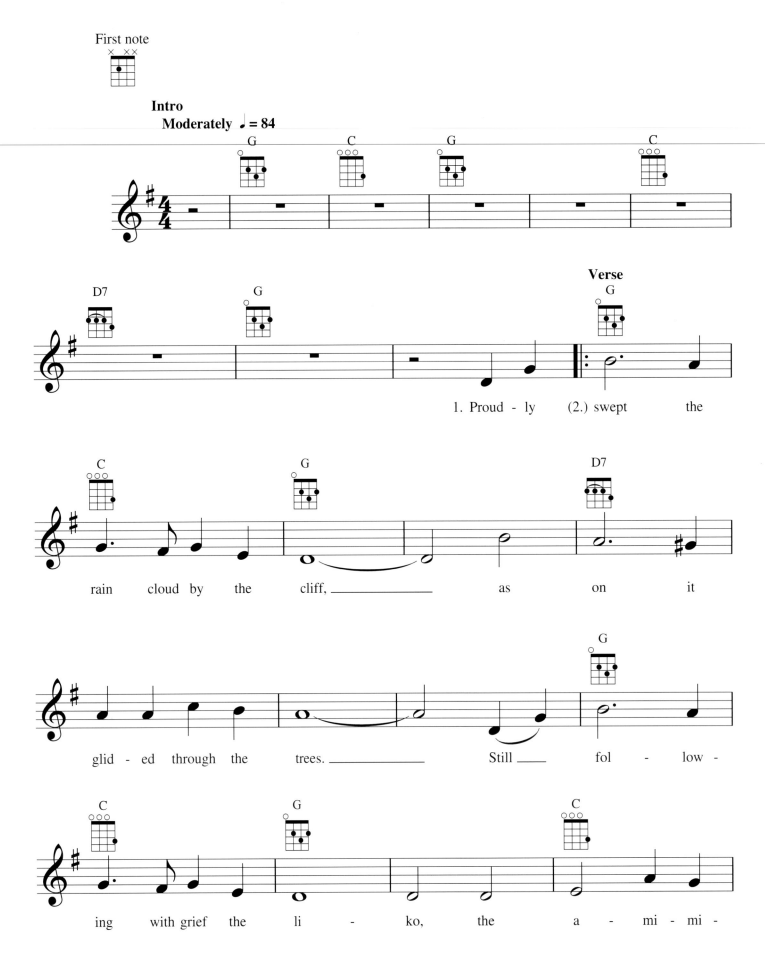

le - mua of the vale. _____ Fare -
A -

Chorus

well to thee, fare - well to thee, thou
lo - ha 'oe, a - lo - ha 'oe, e - ke

charm - ing one who dwells a - mong the bow -
o - na o - na no - ho i ka li -

ers. One fond em - brace be -
po. A fond em - brace a

fore I now de - part, un - til we
ho - 'i a - 'e au, un - til we

1.
2.

meet ___ a - gain. _____ 2. Proud - ly ____
meet ___ a - gain. _____

Blue Hawaii

from the Paramount Picture WAIKIKI WEDDING
Theme from the Paramount Picture BLUE HAWAII
Words and Music by Leo Robin and Ralph Rainger

Harbor Lights

Words and Music by Jimmy Kennedy and Hugh Williams

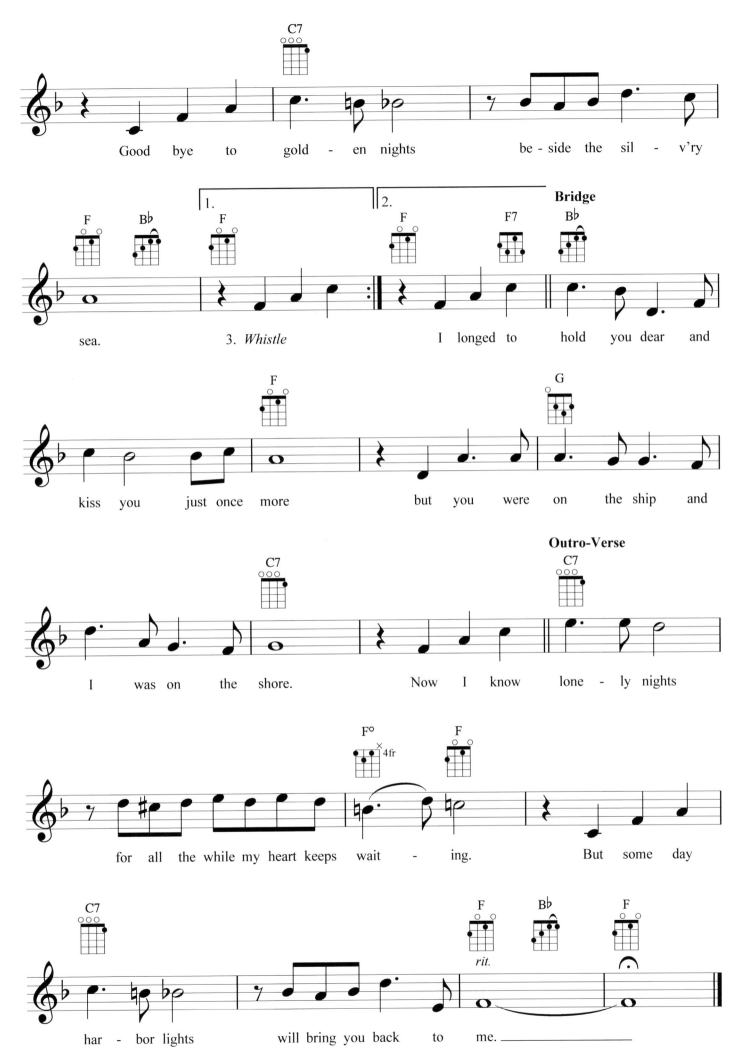

Good bye to gold - en nights be - side the sil - v'ry

1. **2.** **Bridge**

sea. 3. *Whistle* I longed to hold you dear and

kiss you just once more but you were on the ship and

Outro-Verse

I was on the shore. Now I know lone - ly nights

for all the while my heart keeps wait - ing. But some day

rit.

har - bor lights will bring you back to me.

The Hawaiian Wedding Song
(Ke Kali Nei Au)

English Lyrics by Al Hoffman and Dick Manning
Hawaiian Lyrics and Music by Charles E. King

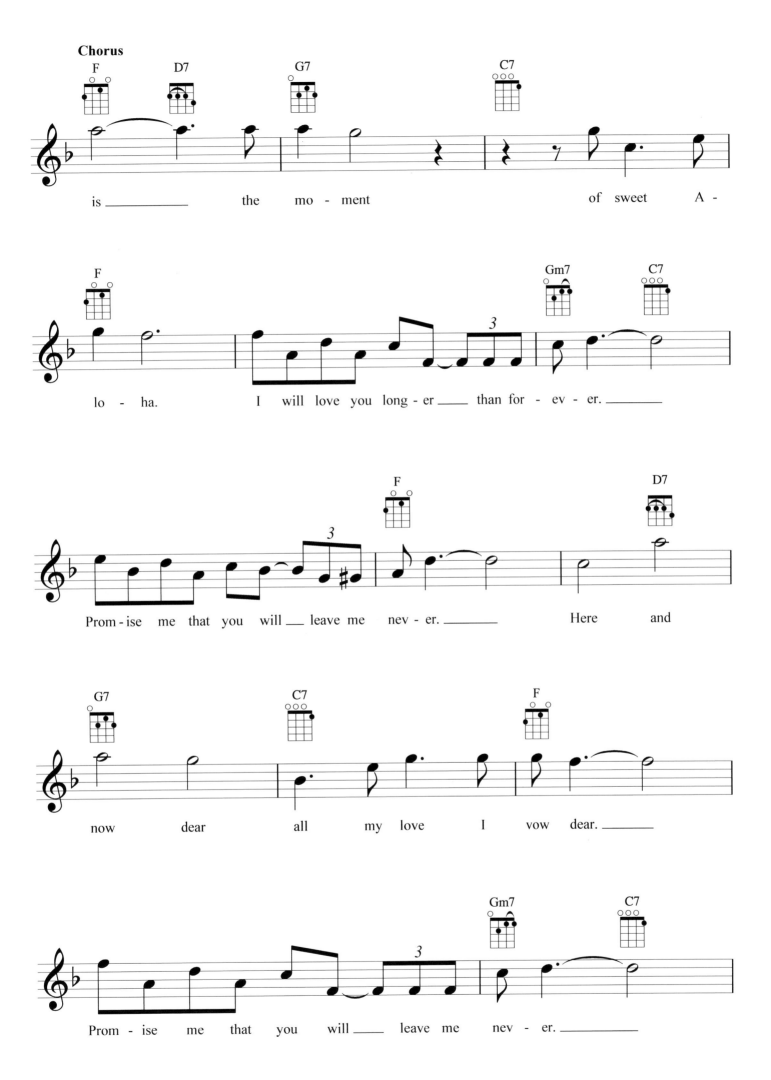

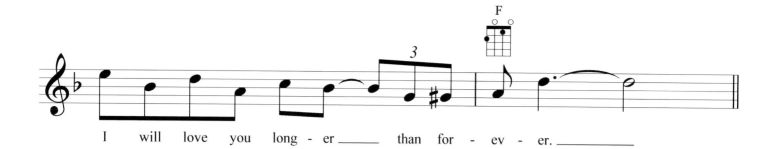

I will love you long - er _____ than for - ev - er. _____

Bridge

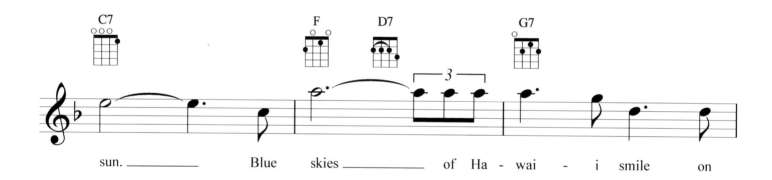

Now that we are one, clouds won't hide the

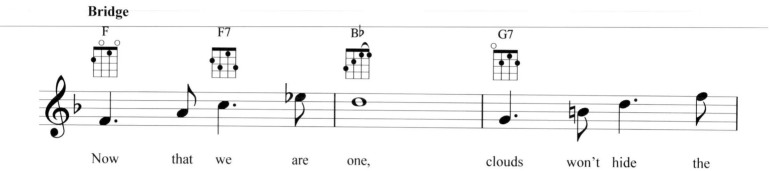

sun. _____ Blue skies _____ of Ha - wai - i smile on

Outro

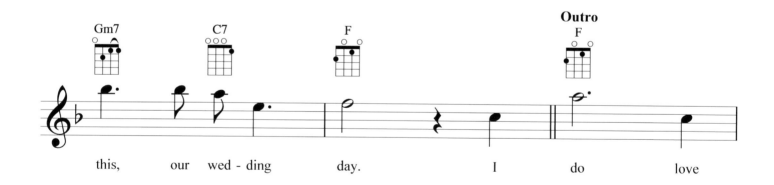

this, our wed - ding day. I do love

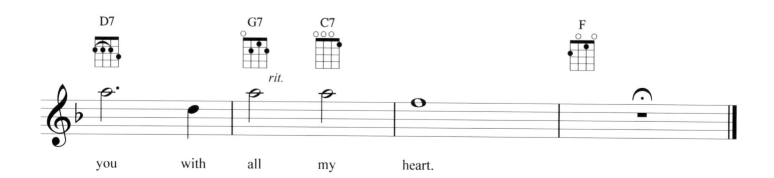

you with all my heart.

Mele Kalikimaka

Words and Music by R. Alex Anderson

land where palm trees sway. _____

Here we know that Christ - mas will be green and bright, ____ the

sun to shine by day and all the stars at night.

Me - le Kal - i - ki - mak - a is Ha - wai - i's way _____ to

say Mer - ry Christ - mas to you.

𝄋 Verse

2. Me - le Kal - i - ki - mak - a is the thing to say _____ on a

bright Ha - wai - ian Christ - mas day. _____

That's the is - land greet - ing that we send to you _____ from the

land where palm tree sway. _____

Here we know that Christ - mas will be green and bright, _____ the

sun to shine by day and all the stars at night. _____

Me - le Kal - i - ki - mak - a is Ha - wai - i's way _____ to

To Coda **Solo-Verse**

say Mer - ry Christ - mas to you.

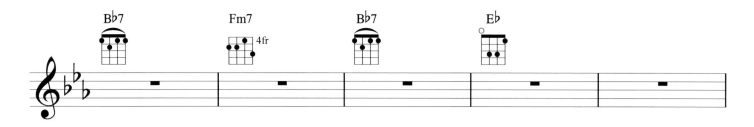

Here we know that Christ - mas will be green and bright, the

sun to shine by day and all the stars at night.

Me - le Kal - i - ki - mak - a is Ha - wai - i's way _____ to

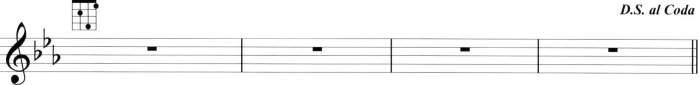

say Mer - ry Christ - mas to you.

Interlude

Bb13

D.S. al Coda

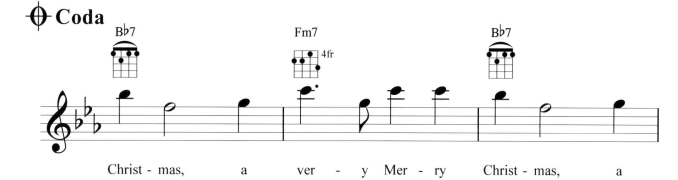

Christ - mas, a ver - y Mer - ry Christ - mas, a

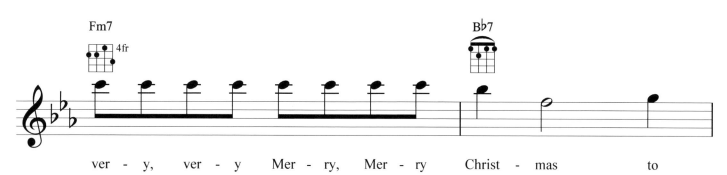

ver - y, ver - y Mer - ry, Mer - ry Christ - mas to

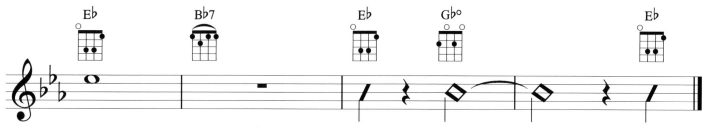

you.

Sleepy Lagoon

Words by Jack Lawrence
Music by Eric Coates

First note

Intro
Slow Waltz ♩ = 69

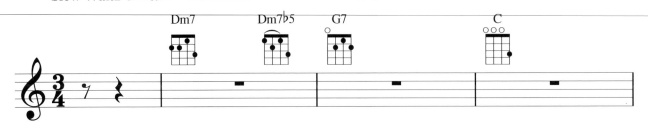

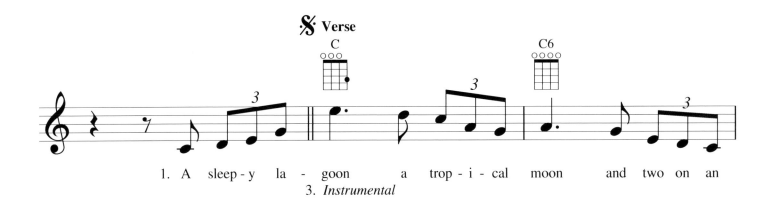

1. A sleep-y la-goon a trop-i-cal moon and two on an
3. *Instrumental*

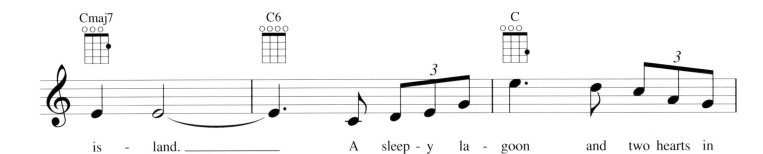

is - land. _____ A sleep-y la-goon and two hearts in

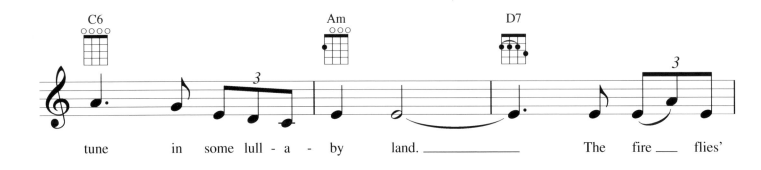

tune in some lull-a-by land. _____ The fire ___ flies'

gleam   re - flects   in   the   stream   they   spark - le   and   shim - mer. _____

____   A   star from   on   high   falls   out   of   the   sky   and   slow - ly   grows

Verse

dim - mer. _____   2., 4. The   leaves from   the   trees   all   dance   in   the

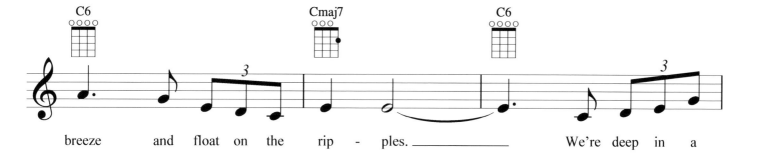

breeze   and   float   on   the   rip - ples. _____   We're   deep   in   a

Tiny Bubbles

Words and Music by Leon Pober

Bridge

So here's to the gold - en moon ___

and here's ___ to the sil - ver sea; ___ and most - ly, here's a toast ___

D.S. al Coda

___ to you and me. ___ 2. Ti - ny

Coda

Verse

3. Ti - ny bub - bles ___ in the wine

make me hap - py, ___ make me feel fine.

Outro

Ti - ny bub - bles _____ make me warm all o - ver

with a feel - in' that I'm gon - na love _____ you till the end _____ of

time, with a feel - in' that I'm gon - na love _____

_____ you, gon - na love you _____ till the end of

time. _____

Sweet Someone

Words by George Waggner
Music by Baron Keyes

HAL•LEONARD®
UKULELE PLAY-ALONG

1. POP HITS
00701451 Book/CD Pack $15.99

3. HAWAIIAN FAVORITES
00701453 Book/Online Audio $14.99

4. CHILDREN'S SONGS
00701454 Book/Online Audio $14.99

5. CHRISTMAS SONGS
00701696 Book/CD Pack $12.99

6. LENNON & MCCARTNEY
00701723 Book/Online Audio $12.99

7. DISNEY FAVORITES
00701724 Book/Online Audio $14.99

8. CHART HITS
00701745 Book/CD Pack $15.99

9. THE SOUND OF MUSIC
00701784 Book/CD Pack $14.99

10. MOTOWN
00701964 Book/CD Pack $12.99

11. CHRISTMAS STRUMMING
00702458 Book/Online Audio $12.99

12. BLUEGRASS FAVORITES
00702584 Book/CD Pack $12.99

13. UKULELE SONGS
00702599 Book/CD Pack $12.99

14. JOHNNY CASH
00702615 Book/Online Audio $15.99

15. COUNTRY CLASSICS
00702834 Book/CD Pack $12.99

16. STANDARDS
00702835 Book/CD Pack $12.99

17. POP STANDARDS
00702836 Book/CD Pack $12.99

18. IRISH SONGS
00703086 Book/Online Audio $12.99

19. BLUES STANDARDS
00703087 Book/CD Pack $12.99

20. FOLK POP ROCK
00703088 Book/CD Pack $12.99

21. HAWAIIAN CLASSICS
00703097 Book/CD Pack $12.99

22. ISLAND SONGS
00703098 Book/CD Pack $12.99

23. TAYLOR SWIFT
00221966 Book/Online Audio $16.99

24. WINTER WONDERLAND
00101871 Book/CD Pack $12.99

25. GREEN DAY
00110398 Book/CD Pack $14.99

26. BOB MARLEY
00110399 Book/Online Audio $14.99

27. TIN PAN ALLEY
00116358 Book/CD Pack $12.99

28. STEVIE WONDER
00116736 Book/CD Pack $14.99

29. OVER THE RAINBOW & OTHER FAVORITES
00117076 Book/Online Audio $15.99

30. ACOUSTIC SONGS
00122336 Book/CD Pack $14.99

31. JASON MRAZ
00124166 Book/CD Pack $14.99

32. TOP DOWNLOADS
00127507 Book/CD Pack $14.99

33. CLASSICAL THEMES
00127892 Book/Online Audio $14.99

34. CHRISTMAS HITS
00128602 Book/CD Pack $14.99

35. SONGS FOR BEGINNERS
00129009 Book/Online Audio $14.99

36. ELVIS PRESLEY HAWAII
00138199 Book/Online Audio $14.99

37. LATIN
00141191 Book/Online Audio $14.99

38. JAZZ
00141192 Book/Online Audio $14.99

39. GYPSY JAZZ
00146559 Book/Online Audio $15.99

40. TODAY'S HITS
00160845 Book/Online Audio $14.99

HAL•LEONARD®
www.halleonard.com